First World War
and Army of Occupation
War Diary
France, Belgium and Germany

52 DIVISION
Headquarters, Branches and Services
Royal Army Veterinary Corps
Deputy Assistant Director Veterinary Services
1 April 1918 - 30 April 1919

WO95/2891/4

The Naval & Military Press Ltd
www.nmarchive.com
Published in association with The National Archives

Published by

The Naval & Military Press Ltd

Unit 10 Ridgewood Industrial Park,

Uckfield, East Sussex,

TN22 5QE England

Tel: +44 (0) 1825 749494

www.naval-military-press.com

www.nmarchive.com

This diary has been reprinted in facsimile from the original. Any imperfections are inevitably reproduced and the quality may fall short of modern type and cartographic standards.

© **Crown Copyright**
Images reproduced by permission of The National Archives, London, England, 2015.

Contents

Document type	Place/Title	Date From	Date To
Heading	WO95/2891/4 Deputy Assistant Director Veterinary Services.		
Heading	52nd Division D.A Dir. Vety Services Apr 1918-Apr 1919		
War Diary	Jaffa	01/04/1918	02/04/1918
War Diary	Surafend	03/04/1918	04/04/1918
War Diary	Alexandria	05/04/1918	11/04/1918
War Diary	Marseilles	17/04/1918	17/04/1918
War Diary	Rue	20/04/1918	27/04/1918
War Diary	Aire	28/04/1918	07/05/1918
War Diary	Villers Au Bois	11/05/1918	28/06/1918
War Diary	Pernes	22/07/1918	22/07/1918
War Diary	Maroeuil	31/07/1918	31/07/1918
War Diary	Pernes	02/08/1918	02/08/1918
War Diary	Maroeuil	02/08/1918	02/08/1918
War Diary	Villers Chatel	16/08/1918	18/08/1918
War Diary	Hermaville	21/08/1918	21/08/1918
War Diary	Bretencourt	22/08/1918	01/09/1918
War Diary	Boiry	03/09/1918	03/09/1918
War Diary	Croiselles	04/09/1918	07/09/1918
War Diary	St. Leger	08/09/1918	17/09/1918
War Diary	Queant	18/09/1918	30/09/1918
War Diary	Bretencourt	01/09/1918	01/09/1918
War Diary	Boiry	03/09/1918	03/09/1918
War Diary	Croiselles	04/09/1918	07/09/1918
War Diary	St. Leger	08/09/1918	17/09/1918
War Diary	Queant	18/09/1918	30/09/1918
War Diary	Graincourt	01/10/1918	02/10/1918
War Diary	Vaulx-Vraucourt	06/10/1918	06/10/1918
War Diary	Le Cauroy	07/10/1918	10/10/1918
War Diary	Chateau D'Acq	19/10/1918	19/10/1918
War Diary	Henin Lietard	20/10/1918	20/10/1918
War Diary	Maison Blanche	22/10/1918	22/10/1918
War Diary	Flines	24/10/1918	24/10/1918
War Diary	Sameon	29/10/1918	18/11/1918
War Diary	Nimy	21/12/1918	23/01/1919
Miscellaneous	Classification Of Animals		
Miscellaneous	D.A.D.V.S 155th Inf. Bde. A.D.M.S	30/12/1918	30/12/1918
Miscellaneous	Classification Of Animals		
War Diary	Nimy	01/03/1919	24/03/1919
War Diary	Soignies	25/03/1919	31/03/1919
War Diary	Soignies Belgium	01/04/1919	20/04/1919
War Diary	Ohligs	01/04/1919	30/04/1919

WO 95/2891/4

Deputy Assistant Director
Veterinary Services

52ND DIVISION

D.A.DIR. VETY SERVICES
APR 1918-APR 1919

WAR DIARY or INTELLIGENCE SUMMARY

Army Form C/2118.

Place	Date	Hour	Summary of Events and Information	Remarks and references to Appendices
JAFFA.	1-4-18		Inspected Mobile Vety Section at SAROMA, & arranged with S.A.V.O. 7th Indian Division stand arrangements the any animals unable to travel when Section out.	
	2-4-18		Left JAFFA for SURAFEND with his Holzers.	
SURAFEND	3-4-18		Mobile Vety Section arrived at SURAFEND from SARONA. Mobile Vety Inspected Mobile Vety Section on arrival. S.V.S. inspected Mobile Vety Section on arrival.	
	4-4-18		Handed in to resources at LUDD all animals Horses readily & which landed in to Alexander. Reported Departure to S.V.S. Left Ludd for Alexandria. Arrived Alexandria.	
ALEXANDRIA	5-4-18			
	8-4-18		Embarked on H.M.T. INDARRA	
	14-4-18		Sailed from Alexandria	

Army Form C. 2118.

WAR DIARY
or
INTELLIGENCE SUMMARY.
(Erase heading not required.)

Vol I.
page VI.

Place	Date	Hour	Summary of Events and Information	Remarks and references to Appendices
MARSEILLES	19.4.18		Disembarked MARSEILLES & entrained for ROUEN	
	20.4.18		Arrived ROUEN.	
	21.4.18		Reported arrival to A.D.V.S. Reserve Army.	
	22.4.18		Whole Hy. Echn. arrived at ROMAINE from Advance Base	
	23.4.18		1st & 2nd Brigade Crew transport ABBEVILLE. Transport left for Lt. Col. Ashley, Capt. Purcell & 2/C Supt. 52"Brigade R.F.A.	
			Disembarked arrival of Reserve Army hy transport	
	24.4.18		reported for duty with 58" Reserve Army	
	25.4.18		Inspected meth. (a) & 1st Reserve Army by tractor. Arrived in ROUE & FAVIERS area.	
	26.4.18		Inspected with a 8 1st Reserve Army R.A. arrived at Port à Grand & Col. LAVIERS.	
	27.4.18		2/W Marshall A.V.C. reported for duty with S.A.C. Left ROUE for AIRE with new Headquarters.	

Army Form C. 2118.

WAR DIARY
or
INTELLIGENCE SUMMARY.
(Erase heading not required.)

Vol I Sheet VII

Place	Date	Hour	Summary of Events and Information	Remarks and references to Appendices
AIRE	28.4.18		Reported arrival at A.D.V.S. XI Corps.	
	29.4.18		Inspected arrival of Sec. Train, 8th Squad Cos. 413 C. R E. M.M.P. at AIRE	
	30.4.18		Inspected Animals 2 /55, /56, /57 Inf Brigade 2 vet & 3rd Field Ambulance. All the animals of the Div. have been drawn from Base transport Depot & Remount Depot ABBEVILLE during the last week. The draught animals with exception are in fair condition. Many show signs of not having been recently heated for this absence there should are hard & the gair patchy, but are on the whole and an average the Riding horses are good & show considerable though many are thin. Adamson Major AVC S.a.S.V.O 52nd Div.	

Army Form C. 2118.

VOLUME XVII
SHEET I
Vol. III

BANK? 50 Division

WAR DIARY
INTELLIGENCE SUMMARY.
(Erase heading not required.)

Instructions regarding War Diaries and Intelligence
Summaries are contained in F. S. Regs., Part II.
and the Staff Manual respectively. Title pages
will be prepared in manuscript.

Place	Date	Hour	Summary of Events and Information	Remarks and references to Appendices
AIRE	1/5/18		Instructed to send A.V.C. Sergeant to Boulogne to accompany Remounts. Found that Duration Sergeant Bradly A.V.C. was accordingly detailed	
	2/5/18		Report to A.D.V.S. XI Corps on Sergeant McNabb attacked by Brigade as inefficient & requested that he be replaced	
	4/5/18		Inspected into the failure of A.D.V.S. XI Corps, horses sent into Mobile Veterinary Section at AIRE from 56 Brigade R.F.A. needed purging. Animals returned to Unit same day.	
	6/5/18		Inquiry accompanied by A.D.V.S. XI Corps to 66 Brigade R.F.A. at FRUGES	
	6/5/18		Found some of the Divisional Headquarters from A.V.C. at VIEUX PONT BOS on transfer to the XIII Corps, and reported arrival at A.D.V.S.	
	7/5/18		Mobile Vety Section arrived at AUX REITS and took over site from the Canadian M.V.S.	

Army Form C. 2118.

WAR DIARY
or
INTELLIGENCE SUMMARY.
(Erase heading not required.)

SHEET II

Instructions regarding War Diaries and Intelligence Summaries are contained in F. S. Regs., Part II. and the Staff Manual respectively. Title pages will be prepared in manuscript.

Place	Date	Hour	Summary of Events and Information	Remarks and references to Appendices
VILLERS AU BOIS	11/3/18		Attended Conference at the office of ADMS XVIII Corps on H/C meal of procedure during adm. operations.	
			Report to ZADOS regarding two Polish R.C.s which were causing alarm to straight armed sentries wearing their coats the same for all harness straps except O.	
	14/3/18		Cases of sarcoptic mange reported by 2nd Sqdn Household Cavalry in L.O. horses belonging to 16th Can Royal when seen. Pencer Patrol. Case was evacuated to Base Hospital. All precautions taken to prevent spread of disease.	
	19/3/18		One other rank's horse transferred from the M.S.D. to XVIII VES	
			XVIII VES branch to receive animals for evacuation.	
	20/3/18		Attended a demonstration as to the method of treatment of Horse and gas Poisoning	
	29/3/18			
	23/3/18		Proceeded on 14 days leave to U.K. Capt MacDonald A.V.C. acting A.D.V.S. during my absence	

Army Form C. 2118.

WAR DIARY
INTELLIGENCE SUMMARY.
(Erase heading not required.)

SHEET III

Place	Date	Hour	Summary of Events and Information	Remarks and references to Appendices
			During the month the animals generally have improved in condition, though many are still poor. Every advantage is being taken of grazing and as more liberal supply of forage has been issued. The 1/1st Lowland Mobile Section was formed in May 1915, the personnel being drawn from the Lowland Veterinary Hospital, Stirling. Embarked for overseas June or 1915 J Adamson Major A.V.C S & 8 Pb. 52nd Div	

D.A.D.V.S.,
52nd DIVISION
No...........
Date: 2/7/16

C. 2118.

WAR DIARY
INTELLIGENCE SUMMARY.
(Erase heading not required.)

VOLUME XVIII
SHEET. I

Place	Date	Hour	Summary of Events and Information	Remarks and references to Appendices
VILLERS AU BOIS	JUNE 1916		During the month the Division has been stationary and transport generally has had little work. On the whole the animals have done well, when in consideration all round — there is now noticeable improvement in condition all round — this is no doubt due to when the R.A. & most animals have not done so well as those of ?amby those and the A.S.C. The probable reason of shortage of labour on the Wagon lines, owing to licence amongst the Personnel of men being employed on other duties. Forage is of fair quality & equal meat has been supplied. Also the animals are forward, and have had plenty of grazing. Check of animals taken 20.6. Total 1520. Chiefly one to Debility, Exhaustion, & Deterioration, Injuries and Sickness. Remounts, 10 R. 21 L.D. 31 H.D. and 1 Fox were received. The H.D. horses are traced stamp & in good condition and the Riders are now of a good quality. On June 28th. E. Battalion left the Division together with Transport, G.A.S. wagons and horses. Rail waking the Establishment up by 135 horses and 78 mules. The Mobile Veterinary Station has evacuated 172 animals belonging to various Units even when in the Area. The Establishment of M.V. Section has now been reduced to 11. The sanctioned having been handed over to other Units. Picking up not stock at an satisfactory condition, the Roads & nails supplied are of fair quality, place on an average about 5 weeks owing to the short stamp of regt. metal. J Adamson Major A.V.C.	

Army Form C. 2118.

WAR DIARY
~~INTELLIGENCE SUMMARY.~~
(Erase heading not required.)

Volume XXIV.
Sheet II

Instructions regarding War Diaries and Intelligence Summaries are contained in F. S. Regs., Part II. and the Staff Manual respectively. Title pages will be prepared in manuscript.

Place	Date	Hour	Summary of Events and Information	Remarks and references to Appendices
			The Mobile Veterinary Section has evacuated 117 animals belonging to various units formations within the area. The horsing on the whole is satisfactory.	

J Adamson Major VC
ODAVS. 52nd Division

D.A.D.V.S.,
52nd DIVISION.
No. M/R
Date 3/5/18

DADVS 52
VOLUME XXIV
SHEET 1

WAR DIARY
INTELLIGENCE SUMMARY
(Erase heading not required.)

Army Form C. 2118.

Instructions regarding War Diaries and Intelligence Summaries are contained in F.S. Regs., Part II. and the Staff Manual respectively. Title pages will be prepared in manuscript.

Place	Date	Hour	Summary of Events and Information	Remarks and references to Appendices
VILLERS AU BOIS	July 1918.		During the first 22 days of the month this Division was stationary and transport was not given too much work, both Locos and mules have marked improvement which is now noticeable in the mules. The horses of R.A. have had on a good deal of condition, and are still far from good. Forage is of fair quality & a full ration has been available. Also a small quantity of Lucerne Cake was supplied & grazing so started.	
PERNES	2nd		On the 22nd the Division was relieved in the Line by the 5th Division & the HQ of the M.V.S. was handed over to 8thDivision M.V.S. The Division moved into G.H.Q Reserve in the PERNES area. The M.V.S. being situated at DIVISION. Practically all animals were in the open & the weather was wet. Forage issued at 8lbs hay, 10lbs Oats to L.D. and 6lbs hay, 15lbs Oats to H.D. No grazing available.	
MARBEUIL	31st		Orders received to proceed to MARBEUIL area to relieve the 1st Canadian Division. During the late manoeuvres animals generally had a trifle run condition, particularly those of the R.H.A. units. That was no doubt due to the hot weather and short hay ration. Also to the fact that for some time before the move they had been tied on boiled hoofs once daily. Strength (Army) 2385 Horses 1326 Mules Newfoss " – " 83 " 18 " due owing to debility, saddle injuries, Lameness & Mange. 58R. 134 L.D. 8P.Horses. 90L.D. 5P. Mules & generally were in good condition, but the Mange on most cases required attention before the animals could be put to work.	

D.A.D.V.S.,
52nd DIVISION.

D.A.D.V.S.,
52nd Division
No. 1
Date 3/9/18

WAR DIARY
or
INTELLIGENCE SUMMARY.
(Erase heading not required.)

VOLUME XXV
SHEET I.

Place	Date	Hour	Summary of Events and Information	Remarks and references to Appendices
PERNES, PARDEVIL.	AUGUST 2nd 1918.		Moved with D.H.Q. to Pernes & took over from the D. of Savernak Division. Mobile Vety Section located at Pernes.	
VILLERS-CHATEL	"	16.	Moved with D.H.Q. & Mobile Vety Section into G.H.Q. reserve at Villers Chatel.	
	"	16.	H Corps. Mobile Vety Section moved to Agnieres.	
HERMAVILLE	"	21	Moved into D.H.Q. at Hermaville.	
BRETENCOURT	"	22	established in collecting station. Mobile Vety Section moved to Hauquetin.	
	"	20	Dumbar moved into station.	
	"	24	Mobile Vety Section moved to Bavincourt.	
	"	25	" " " " Bretencourt	
	"	27	Collecting Stn moved to H.30.d near Mercatel. During the month the rate of forage issued was 10/10.6½ lbs & the animals generally were worked extremely hard & are mostly in low condition.	
			Remounts received during the month - no horses "missed". Being on the whole - satisfactory. Wastage in the month - horses, mules 23 due chiefly to Shell Fire (R.H.) Injuries.	

J Bannerman. Major A.V.C.
D.A.D.V.S. 52 Division.

WAR DIARY or INTELLIGENCE SUMMARY

Army Form C. 2118.

VOLUME XXVI   SHEET I

Instructions regarding War Diaries and Intelligence Summaries are contained in F. S. Regs., Part II. and the Staff Manual respectively. Title pages will be prepared in manuscript.

Place	Date	Hour	Summary of Events and Information	Remarks and references to Appendices
BRETENCOURT.	SEPT. 1918.	1st	Division in Action. Moved from Bulencourt to advanced Collecting Post Nr BOIRY (S.6.d. Sh.51.B) Mobile Vety. Section moved from Bulencourt to Boisleux-au-Mont. (S.9.d.2.1.)	
BOIRY.	"	3rd	Moved with Collecting Post to CROISELLES.	
CROISILLES.	"	4th	Mobile Vety. Section moved to CROISELLES. (T.34.D.5.5.) Collecting Post established at C.3.B.5.5.	
"	"	5th	Mobile Vety. Section moved back to Nr BOIRY. (S.6.d.)	
"	"	6th	Battle casualties for W.E. 5-9-18. 63 animals killed and 29 wounded, by shellfire. Division rested and came into support.	
"	"	7th	Opened R.P.D. at St. LEGER.	
"	"	—	General Artillery Orders recalls the administration of 5 yrs. Nr. A.G.H.S. Collecting Post themes at BULLECOURT (C.3.B.5.5) to deal with R.A. animals for evacuation.	
St. LEGER.	"	8th	Capt. J.S. Purcell A.M.C. evacuated and rejoined on duty.	
"	"	12th	Mobile Vety. Section moves to St. LEGER. (B.19.a.4.8) Battle casualties for W.E. 12-9-18. 12 animals killed and 4 wounded by bombs and shell fire R.A. casualties with syphilis. 14 horses and 4 mules killed. Division relieve 57th Div. in the line	
"	"	14th	R.A. reports the Division...	
"	"	15th	Instructed R.A. animals and mules that are horses or mules reinventorial that 12 should be unequitted from 1 if Luvay.	
"	"	16th	Capt. J.S. Purcell awarded immediate M.C. recently wounded.	
"	"	—	Moved to QUEANT (D.Y.A.S.F.) with C.O.	
"	"	17th	Mobile Vety. Section moves to HENDECOURT. (Division ell inoperable and evacuationable ist VY chevaux le son BOIRY.)	
"	"	18th	Mobile Vety. Section moves to ECOUST.	
"	"	19th	Battle casualties for W.E. 19-9-18. 21 animals killed and 26 wounded by shellfire.	
QUEANT.	"	23rd	Entering Post established at QUEANT. (D.Y.a.5.F.)	
"	"	26th	Collecting Post established Nr QUEANT.	
"	"	26th	Battle casualties for W.E. 27-9-18. 24 animals killed and 22 wounded by shell fire.	
"	"	24th	Mobile Vety Section moves to LAGNICOURT. (I.C.c. central)	
"	"	26th		
"	"	29th	Collecting Post moves to E.26. d. Lieut. R. Smith R.A.V.C. admitted for study sick base J.S. Purcell to hospital	

Army Form C. 2118.

WAR DIARY
of
INTELLIGENCE SUMMARY.
(Erase heading not required.)

Instructions regarding War Diaries and Intelligence Summaries are contained in F.S. Regs., Part II. and the Staff Manual respectively. Title pages will be prepared in manuscript.

VOLUME XXVI
SHEET II

Place	Date	Hour	Summary of Events and Information	Remarks and references to Appendices
QUEANT	Sept 1918	30th	During the month there has been hard mental exposure. Most of the R.A. who have been in the line continuously. The weather has been cold and miserably how last a little exertion. Hay ration on the 15th inst was reduced 1½ lbs. per animal, being now 11 lbs. for H.D. & Cav. & 9 lbs. for L.D. Since that date a small quantity of green clover has been supplied on most days, varying from 1lb. to 3 lbs. per animal. Drawing water of animals on arriving on 21/20 and march of artillery and that mounted units not adequately sufficient for needs. 160 carcasses of animals have been examined after evacuation as cases of too bad enough as they were too weak & exhausted/of cattle made and and which contained other them not of high grade. The veterinary officers available. Strong — Subaltern 17 V.S. has inoculated 253 horses and 65 mules during the month. Remounts received. 163 horses 225 mules.	J Adamson Major A.V.C. D.A.D.V.S. 52nd Div

D.A.D.V.S.
52nd DIVISION.
No. 629
Date 1-10-18

Army Form C. 2118.

WAR DIARY
or
INTELLIGENCE SUMMARY.
(Erase heading not required.)

VOLUME XXVI
SHEET I
3/10/18

Instructions regarding War Diaries and Intelligence Summaries are contained in F. S. Regs., Part II. and the Staff Manual respectively. Title pages will be prepared in manuscript.

Place	Date	Hour	Summary of Events and Information	Remarks and references to Appendices
BRIENCOURT	SEPT. 1918.	1st	Divisional Relief. Heavy Arty. Section moves from Authieul to Bienvillers-aux-Bois (S.9.d.2.3.) Mobile Vety.	
		3rd	Arrived at billeting areas at CROISELLES	
BOIRY CROISELLES		3rd	Hy Ay 14th Battery moves to CROISELLES (T.24.b.3x)	
		4th	Divl'l Boss established at C.3.b.55	
		5th	Mobile Vety Section moves to MRBOIRY (36.L.)	
		5th	Spath Ammunition for A.E. 5-9-18. 62 rounds killed and 29 rounds of shrapnel	
		6th	Divisional H.Q. moves forward	
		7th	Advanced H.Q. to St LEGER.	
ST LEGER		7th	Divisional Artillery came under the administration of XVIIth Corps.	
		7th	Hy Ay 9th Section DULLECOURT (O.3.b.5.1.) 7.E and 10.6 R.A. rounds for bombardment	
		8th	Area of H.L. Bdes A.D.C. returns and movs in at dusk.	
		10th	Mobile Vety Section moves to ST LEGER (B.Y.2.48)	
		13th	3/31st casualties for M.B. 13.9.18, 13 rounds killed and 7 wounded by bombs and shell fire	
			No casualties 14th 15/9/18 - 14 horse and 17 mules killed	
		14th	Divisions relieve 5th Divis. in the line	
		14th	Hy Ay returns the Division	
		16th	Battle R.A. rounds and horse class are less fresh condition, recommend are to also to be evacuated from Divisory.	
		16.45	Batho. R.A. Reserve ammunition with casualty round.	
		16.45	Corps Hy Bosst assumed control	
		14.5	Moved to QUEANT (BY R.S.Y) NIB. C.5.6.	
		14.5	Mobile Vety Section moves to NERDECOURT (N.19.d.5.4) several rs and mules is evacuated returning there day towards are in front.	
		16th	Mobile Vety Section moves to ETOUST.	
QUEANT		19th	Battle casualties for M.B. 19-9-18, 24 rounds killed and 26 wounded by shell fire.	
		23rd	Battery Post reestablished	
		26th	Battery Boss established H.E. QUEANT. (D.Y.a.S.R.)	
		24th	Battle casualties for M.B. 3-9-18, 3 rounds killed and 23 wounded by shell fire	
		29th	Mobile Vety Section moves to LAGNICOURT. (L.6.c.central.)	
		29th	Arrive rely. Section moves to E.3.5.a.	
		30th	Appendix Documents, A, B, C,D,E. and DD for Sept. also Maps, F.G. Parade is Location.	

Army Form C. 2118.

Instructions regarding War Diaries and Intelligence Summaries are contained in F. S. Regs., Part II. and the Staff Manual respectively. Title pages will be prepared in manuscript.

WAR DIARY
or
INTELLIGENCE SUMMARY.
(Erase heading not required.)

VOLUME XXVI
SHEET II

Place	Date	Hour	Summary of Events and Information	Remarks and references to Appendices
QUEANT	31st 1918	30th	During the month animals especially those of the R.A. who have been in the line continuously. Weather has been cold and the mud covered jersey have had a settling condition. H.Q. for H.D. Since the 15th inst was relieved 15 the transport, having now little for H.D. & saying from L+S. I.B. as usual. Watering arrangements in carry areas are unsatisfactory and have accumulated and attempt supplies for second O.C. squadrons R.A animals had long hours and have to try and water the out lying districts. This is a length of many of carrier the area where could have been water troughs at short ends. Shoeing — Satisfactory M.V.S. has evacuated 253 horses and 65 mules during the month. Remounts received. 163 Horses 225 Mules.	

Adamson Major A.V.C.
S A V S
52nd Div

Army Form C. 2118

WAR DIARY
or
INTELLIGENCE SUMMARY.
(Erase heading not required.)

D.A.D.V.S.
52nd DIVISION.

VOLUME XXVII. SHEET 1.

Place	Date	Hour	Summary of Events and Information	Remarks and references to Appendices
GRAINCOURT	OCTOBER 1st 1918.		Moved to GRAINCOURT, where a Collecting Post was established. M.V.S. moved to E.23.d. central. ARMOEVRES.	
	2nd		Batte Casualties N.E. 2/10/18. 34 animals killed and 22 wounded.	
VAULX-VRAUCOURT	6th		Moved to VAULX-VRAUCOURT.	
LE CAUROY	7th		Division moved into rest. Two R.A. who are attached to XVIII Corps	
	10th		A case of Foot & Mouth Disease occured at IZEL LES-HAMEAUX which was investigated & one cow was found to be suspected, others show signs of having recently recovered from the disease.	
CHATEAU D'ACQ	19th		Batte Casualties N.E. 10/10/18. 9 animals killed and 2 destroyed. Moved to CHATEAU D'ACQ.	
HENIN LIETARD	20th		" " HENIN-LIETARD.	
MAISON BLANCHE	22nd		M.V.S. moved to FOSSOULIERS HENIN LIETARD.	
			Moved to MAISON BLANCHE.	
FLINES	24th		" " FLINES.	
			M.V.S. moved to WARENDIN.	
CAMEON	29th		Casualties N.E. 24/10/18. 10 Horses killed, one wounded & one mule wounded by shell fire. All Army animals belonging to R.A. units who composed the Division during the week. Moved to Cameon.	
	28th		M.V.S. moved to BEUVRY.	

Army Form C. 2118.

WAR DIARY
or
INTELLIGENCE SUMMARY.
(Erase heading not required.)

VOLUME XXVII
Sheet II

D.A.D.V.S.
52nd DIVISION
Date 3/11/18

Place	Date	Hour	Summary of Events and Information	Remarks and references to Appendices
SIMEON	Oct	3	Casualties 15/9/18. 18 Horses and 6 Mules killed and 10 Horses & 1 Mule wounded by Shell fire.	
		28	Lt. H.W. Marshall attached 9 Brigade RFA, admitted to Hospital suffering from internal ear disease.	
			From October 29th the Division was not employed in operations & the condition of animals generally improved. Forage was of fair quality & during the latter part of the month grazing was to some extent available. Forty seven cases of Debility have been evacuated. These were in aged animals in the majority of them came from R.E. Coys & M.G. Battalion.	
			Shoeing except in R.H. is satisfactory. The R.H. having been detached from the Division received no shoes & nails for a period of two weeks & the shoeing is now in need of immediate attention.	
			Draught horses are being shipped Base Depôt. M.V.S. Loo evacuated 187 horses and 40 mules during the month. Remounts received — 150 horses and 19 mules.	

J Adamson
Major AVC
D.A.D.V.S. 52 Division

Army Form C.2118.
52nd DIVISION.
4/12/18.

WAR DIARY
INTELLIGENCE SUMMARY.
(Erase heading not required.)

Place	Date	Hour	Summary of Events and Information	Remarks and references to Appendices
SEMEON	NOVEMBER 1918. 8th		A.F.S. moved to BOUDOUR.	
	9th		Moved to PERUWELZ.	
			" " SIRAULT	
		10th	Casualties OR 14/11/18 12 horses and 4 mules killed & three had to have been destroyed.	
	11.		Moved to NIMY.	
	12.			
			We had two units of the Division the Canadian & animals that were uncared for. sick or suffering and unacc— for duty. W/horses animals. Ran 22 kms.	
			Owing to the early day of the war and so returned to Bancroft difficulties. Was unaware of their travel went & B. were necessarily complete.	
			Remounts received during the march by road 43 miles	

Army Form C. 2118.

Instructions regarding War Diaries and Intelligence Summaries are contained in F. S. Regs., Part II. and the Staff Manual respectively. Title pages will be prepared in manuscript.

WAR DIARY
or
INTELLIGENCE SUMMARY.
(Erase heading not required.)

VOLUME XXVIII
SHEET L.

4/12/18.

Place	Date	Hour	Summary of Events and Information	Remarks and references to Appendices
SENEON.	NOVEMBER 1918. 8th		M.T.O. moved to BOUDOUR	
	9th		Moved to PERUWELZ	
	10th		" " SIRAULT	
			Casualties 10/11/18 12 horses and 4 mules killed by shell fire	
	11		9.15 Horse Lines to be reinforced	
	13.		Moved to NIMY.	
			The last two weeks of the month it consisted of animal transport. Rly Const & Debrity was generally improved. Rations chiefly again arrived from R.O.P. units. Heavy - The early part of the month the rations to transport supplies. The arrears of shoes & nails were considerable. Later on ordinary supplies.	
			Reinforcements received during the month. 37 Lv. OR 42 m.u.C.	Fresh AVC a.a.a.O.E. 5ino Division

WAR DIARY
INTELLIGENCE SUMMARY
(Erase heading not required.)

Place	Date	Hour	Summary of Events and Information	Remarks and references to Appendices
NIMY	DECEMBER 1918.		During the month the horses has been stabled in the	
			Majority of the animals were in stable. Forage was of fair	
			quality, issued at the rate of 10 lb of oats & 8 lb of hay per	
			day & light draught animals, there has been a marked	
			improvement in condition of animals, this is most noticable in	
			the horses met R.A. which is (My Lane had cable over	
			head round tub.	
	24.		Mobile Veterinary Section moved from BOUDOUR to	
			MAISIERES (Nostus) K.11 a 9.6	
	27		D.D.V.S. 1st Army inspected Command for Cooking up Veg	
			Ration at MONS & S.D. Gds Blndr arrived next door	
			of the In were Cart for Sale.	
	28.		Received Instructions from Army D.V.S. to hire Vet Board to inspect &	
			Class unclas. R.A.Y.C. & 9th Fus horses & cog & Lancashire	

(A7993) Wt. W12839/M1093. 750,000. 1/17. D.D. & L. Ltd. Forms/C.2118/4

Army Form C. 2118.

WAR DIARY
or
INTELLIGENCE SUMMARY.
(Erase heading not required.)

Vol XXIX
July

Place	Date	Hour	Summary of Events and Information	Remarks and references to Appendices
MIMY	DECEMBER 1918			
	30		Fishing Boat arrived at D.H.2 & inspected. Crew of D.H.2 inspected the R.E. & M.M.P.	
	30		Board inspected & reported having 52 rats & ?? ??	
			During the month no cases of Mange occurred. Sheep Satisfactory.	
			Wastage level 1 Sabotaged 1 Evacuated 21 Recovered received Nil	

J. Anderson Major
S.A.V.S.
52nd Division

WAR DIARY
INTELLIGENCE SUMMARY

Army Form C. 2118.

WD/8/52
XXX
Sheet 98
11

Place	Date	Hour	Summary of Events and Information	Remarks and references to Appendices
NIMY	JANUARY		During the month the Division has been stationary both while at Nivelles and have done well & improved in condition & rifle. A fair amount of work has been done by the transport & animals and these have to help the civilians to do general carting & farm work.	
			All animals have been inspected & arranged to a Board of Veterinary Officers in accordance with the attached instruction through out the 18th inst. Copy of return called for & covered by the 18th inst. attached.	
			Attended Veterinary Board & inspected released animals of 52nd Army Field Ashley Brigade & of clairiges & Battersed.	
	20.		Issued instructions for all animals of Group V & L to be with Mathews also Hong Group Z passed on returned	

Army Form C. 2118.

WAR DIARY
or
INTELLIGENCE SUMMARY.
(Erase heading not required.)

Instructions regarding War Diaries and Intelligence Summaries are contained in F. S. Regs., Part II. and the Staff Manual respectively. Title pages will be prepared in manuscript.

Place	Date	Hour	Summary of Events and Information	Remarks and references to Appendices
NIMY	JANUARY 25		Welcome hut & all Group S Arrivals completed on Branden. 50 Arrivals cast of S.S. H.T. Army for Rehming Leave. Col. J. Aucher in M.O.A.S. During the month 29 Arrivals were sent for to 19,646 off slaughter after Rebels + M.O.P.S + Anti-C. Strum war sent abroad. Wartops evacuated 109. Sick & Injured 10 incl 16 Clerks 5 Arrivals whose are included with 29 shown above 40 Group S Arrivals left the R.A. for Base. Rope + San Grds very satisfactory.	

J Alderson Major
S+S+S
52nd Div

(A7692). Wt. W12839/M.1295. 750,000. 1/17. D. D. & L., Ltd. Forms/C.2118 14.

Classification of Animals

52nd Div. Unit.

ANIMALS.	HORSES				MULES.		
Class	Riding	L.D.	H.D.	Total	L.D.	Pack	Total
Group. A	202	230	75	507	439	35	474
Group. B	101	101	34	236	138	—	138
Group. C	93	168	39	240	70	—	70
Group. C	442	508	273	1223	538	60	598
Group. D	6	—	1	7	16	1	17.

```
D.A.D.V.S.            155th Inf. Bde.     A.D.M.S.
Camp Commdt.          156th Inf. Bde.     D.A.P.M.
Div. Signal Coy.      157th Inf. Bde.     Div. Train.
C.R.E.
```
----

1. On demobilization, all horses and mules of the British Armies in France, including those with Colonial Contingents, are to be classified and marked, in order that they may be disposed of to the best advantage.

2. This will entail examination by Veterinary Boards, followed by selection by Remount Officers.

3. It has been decided to proceed at once with the Examination by Veterinary Boards.

4. The Board of Officers detailed to inspect all animals in this Division will be composed as follows:-
    President ... D.A.D.V.S.
    Members   ... O.C., 1/1st Low. Mob. Vet. Section.
                    V.O. i/c Unit whose animals are
                         under inspection.

5. This Veterinary Board will inspect all animals in the Division and classify them as regards age and soundness in the following groups:-
    A. Practically sound and between the ages of 5 and 8 years, inclusive.
    B. Practically sound and between the ages of 9 and 12 years inclusive.
    C. Fit for work, but over 12 years or permanently unsound.
    D. Only fit either for sale to butchers, or for slaughter for conversion into By-Products.

6. All the animals will be scissor clipped on the near saddle with the letter of the group to which they are assigned.

7. On completion of classifying the animals of the Division, the D.A.D.V.S. will render a Return to this Office on the attached pro forma

8. The programme for the week commencing 30th December will be as follows:-
    Monday.   ... 1000 Div. H.Q.
                   1100 M.M.P.
                   1400 52nd Div. Signal Coy.
           The Board will visit the stables and inspect
                   these animals.

    Tuesday   ... 0930 Div. Train.
           Animals will be visited in stables.

    Thursday....   0930 155th Inf. Brigade.
                   1100 410th Field Coy R.E.
                   1200 1/3rd Low. Field Amb.

        Friday/

2.

Friday	...	0930	156th Inf. Brigade.
		1100	412th Field Coy R.E.
		1200	1/1st Low. Field Amb.
Saturday	...	0930	157th Inf. Brigade.
		1100	413th Field Coy R.E.
		1200	1/2nd Low. Field Amb.

9.   The G.Os.C of the Brigades concerned will wire to this Office (repeating to D.A.D.V.S., C.R.E., and A.D.M.S.) by 1200 on the day previous to the inspection of animals of their Brigade Group, giving the location of the site selected for the inspection.

10.   In the event of any of the animals being at work or not available, for the inspection by the Board, a future date will be arranged for their inspection, but as many animals as possible should be produced for inspection on the dates laid down.

30th December 1918.

E.F. Mullin-Barrett.
Major,
D.A.Q.M.G, 52nd (LOWLAND) DIVISION.

PRO FORMA

RETURN OF ANIMALS EXAMINED BY VETERINARY BOARD.

(First Army 41/45 Q.A.)

Division.	Group A.	Group B.	Group C.	Group D.	Mares 𝜋

..............Date.   ....Signature.

Transportation Animals

ANIMALS.	HORSES.				MULES.		
Class	Riding	P.D	4.D	Total	4.D	Pack	Total
Group A	21	133	16	180	78	68	
Group B	4			80	7	17	
Group C-	13	58	5	76	9	9	
Group C	33	271	10	314	65	63	
Group D	1	2		3			
Group D-		1		1			

Army Form C. 2118.

WAR DIARY
or
INTELLIGENCE SUMMARY.
(Erase heading not required.)

Army Form C. 2118.

Vol XXXII
ADVS 52D
SHEET I
14 MC/13

Place	Date	Hour	Summary of Events and Information	Remarks and references to Appendices
MARCH				
NIMY	1		During the first 24 days of the month the Division remained stationary at NIMY.	
	2		100 "Z" Class animals were despatched to Rouen	
	4		10 mules were sent to 22 V.E.S.	
	"		246 "Z" remounts were despatched to ROUEN.	
	6		A Bath was established when 147 Z class animals were also by station	
	"		260 "Z" Class animals despatched to Rouen	
	7		A.D.S. NIB administration Reforms and Contingents Z Depôts mixing to shortage of Forage - Removal took place then condition being to shortage of forage. Hay supply is very short. General Health - Good	
	10		4. R. "Z" Class + 65 A D Z Class were sent to 20 Cahie M.T. Coy move.	
	11		121 "Z" Class animals were sent to 20 Coy V.E.S, and were inoculated 18th + 19th " " station Receiving great forces	
	12		100 R. Class Horses were also now despatched to Rouen	
	13		Sale of Long Nigs	
	14		Various Veterinary administration - Reception of Animals - Four General Health Good. Forage - Fair Quality	
	"		16 Cavalry Cobs despatched	
	"		12 Y/M To Rose.	
	15		34 X LD animals despatched to Montrepon	
	"		344 animals to Rouen by Train "Z" Class	
	"		60 "X" LD Animals Transferred to 14 Mob. R.L.A	
	"		100 X LD Animal transported to 49th Division at Section Valenciennes	
	19		41 X LD animals to HAVRE by Train	
	20		121 Z animals sent to ROUEN by Train	
	21		346 X class mules for Motor Coy 85659 ME.	

Army Form C. 2118.

WAR DIARY
or
INTELLIGENCE SUMMARY.
(Erase heading not required.)

Instructions regarding War Diaries and Intelligence Summaries are contained in F.S. Regs., Part II. and the Staff Manual respectively. Title pages will be prepared in manuscript.

Place	Date	Hour	Summary of Events and Information	Remarks and references to Appendices
MARCH				
NIMY	23		26 "Z" Animals were sent to ROUEN	
	24		9/ Lieut M.V.S. moved to 66 Rue de BRAINE SOIGNIES	
	"		95 'X' Animals to Lager to Envoy	
SOIGNIES	25		Remount posted to SOIGNIES offices at 66 Rue de BRAINE	
	25		43 X Animals to HAVRE	
	29		Major Johnson M.C.A.A.M.V.S. proceeded to U.K. for demobilisation. Lieut. E. Macklellan	
	"		V.C. joined V.S. took up the duties of A.D.V.S.	
			Capt. J. M. Heath R.A.V.C. etc 5.7.19 his trans Zinnebrook to R.A. Yorkshire also	
	28		13 R.P.+ 55 Animals sent to HAVES	
	29		19 Z mourning and other animals were despatched to BOULOGNE	
			5 R.A.V.C. Officers and 527 other ranks selected for retention on service of the machinery	
			of mobilisation and granted full demob status under Army Order 54 of 1919	
			34 N.C.O. + men R.A.V.C. were retained for retention and promotion for Regular	
			Engt. A. Jackson R.A.V.C. proceeded to U.K. for demobilisation	
			During the latter half of the month 2 Lieut. W.R. York R.G.A. and C.O. 2 other ranks	
			proceeded on U.K. for demobilisation.	
			Lieut B. Groves A.M.C. was posted to 9.R. York R.G.A. for the purpose of proceeding to	
			U.K. with 9th batch of that unit	
			The following animals Were Evacuated Sick	50
			" " " Died	2
			" " " Destroyed	16
			" " " " "	2

R.W. Macklellan
Lieut. S.R. 52nd Division

Army Form C. 2118.

DADVS 52 Vol XXXIII

No. 14

WAR DIARY
or
INTELLIGENCE SUMMARY.
(Erase heading not required.)

Instructions regarding War Diaries and Intelligence Summaries are contained in F.S. Regs., Part II. and the Staff Manual respectively. Title pages will be prepared in manuscript.

Place	Date	Hour	Summary of Events and Information	Remarks and references to Appendices
April SOIGNIES BELGIUM	1/4		The Div. H.Q. remained at Soignies all April. Orders were received for the refitting of 4 Pks 1/, 10 or B. & 20 Mob Vet Sections from those were issued on 1/4/19. 1 no. proceeded K 2Ld for demobilisation same day.	
	2		2 OR & 1 Hol: yo: Rank G. from 1/2 or 018	
	4		4 OR & " "	
	10		Animals of 2 K Bde Rtt were dispatched K.72 ems Luzet 5B, Gratin Rt 416 strength 4 Bde Rtt proceeded to H.Q. was demobilisation 11 Surplus Rs of V.C. Sy. & were reported to 108 Veterinary Hospital Calais	
	12		for the purpose of transhipment to blighth Reported & 42 mJ 4 in French Army for sale	
	16		Valuable Sy C infected & 26.1 O/cary ablego A.T.Hosp Valenciennes probably	
	26		A on Transporter m 29 to Vet Hosp Calais rapt Demobilization	

Encircled Sgd. ? Rapad

D.A.D.V.S.
52nd DIVISION
No. ....
Date 2/5/19

10 5 45

[signature]

DADVS 52 [signature]

Army Form C. 2118.

WAR DIARY
INTELLIGENCE SUMMARY.
(Erase heading not required.)

Instructions regarding War Diaries and Intelligence Summaries are contained in F.S. Regs. Part II. and the Staff Manual respectively. Title pages will be prepared in manuscript.

Place	Date	Hour	Summary of Events and Information	Remarks and references to Appendices
OH & I. G. S.	1-4-19 to 15-4-19		During these dates there was no D.A.D.V.S of this Division. The Veterinary Officer who was acting D.A.D.V.S. apparently did not keep a diary, but so far as I can ascertain nothing of importance occurred	G.H.Q.
"	16-4-19		Reported my arrival for duty as D.A.D.V.S. to A.D.V.S. Corps.	G.H.Q.
"	17-4-19		Went to 11 Corps H.Q., saw A.D.V.S. and discussed with him various matters in connection with the Veterinary Services in the Corps and Division. Went to M.V.S. and inspected that unit.	G.H.Q.
"	18-4-19		Attended to cases under treatment at D.H.Q. A.D.S., called and went to M.V.S. and inspected animals then awaiting evacuation.	G.H.Q.
"	19-4-19		Held conference with Veterinary Officers in the Division. Gave instructions as to various matters in connection with their duties, and arranged Veterinary charges	G.H.Q.
"	"		normal routine	G.H.Q.
"	20-4-19		Attended to cases under treatment at D.H.Q. Inspected animals of 9th Signal Co. R.E.	G.H.Q.
"	21-4-19		Went to SOLING EN and met Captain Graham R.A.V.C. and inspected the following units which he was in charge of :- 57 & 58 Bde. R.F.A., 26 Hy.Bde, 105 Coy R.A.S.C, and Hd. Qrs.	G.H.Q.
"	22-4-19		Traffic control	G.H.Q.
"	23-4-19		Attended to cases under treatment at D.H.Q. Went to M.V.S. Inspected with Captain Clay R.A.V.C. "A" & "B" Batteries 51st Bde. R.F.A. of which units he was in Veterinary charge of.	G.H.Q.
"	24-4-19		Went to M.V.S. and inspected animals awaiting evacuation.	G.H.Q.
"	25-4-19		Went to M.V.S. and inspected with Captain J. S. Clay R.A.V.C. "A" and "B" Batteries 51st Bde. R.F.A., of which units he was in Veterinary charge of.	G.H.Q.

WAR DIARY
or
INTELLIGENCE SUMMARY.
(Erase heading not required.)

Army Form C. 2118.

D.A.D.V.S. LOWLAND DIVISION.

Date 1.5.19

Place	Date	Hour	Summary of Events and Information	Remarks and references to Appendices
D.H.Q.G.S.	26-4-19		Met Captain J.W. Knaggs and inspected with him the following units viz. is in Veterinary Charge of :- D.A.C, 28th Inf. Bde, 107 Coy R.A.S.C, 63rd Coy R.B., 2/1 East Lancashire Field Ambulance.	J.N.1.
"	27-4-19		Normal routine	J.N.2.
"	28-4-19		Met with A.D.V.S. Corps to inspect remounts of 5W: Bde, R.F.A. all arrived. Nothing very wrong. Inspected horse of 27 Field Ambulance which was nothing wrong.	J.N.2.
"	29-4-19		Met Captain J. Graham R.A.V.C. and inspected with him the following units which he was in Veterinary Charge of :- 64 Field Coy. R.E., 90th Field Coy. R.E. and 2 Companies of the 16. H.L.I. (Pioneers). The stable management in these units left much to be desired.	J.N.2.
"	30-4-19		Paid two Staff Captain No 2 Inf. Bde. with reference to the erection of a Tent at Ca. No. V.S. to house a kneesorm and outlying respresentation for the Personnel. The existing arrangement was very unsatisfactory. Interviewed O.C. Brit. Trains with a view to their arranging instructor to moving animals.	J.N.2.
"	30-4-19			

J. D. Taylor
Major R.A.V.C.
D.A.D.V.S. Lowland Division.

www.ingramcontent.com/pod-product-compliance
Lightning Source LLC
Chambersburg PA
CBHW081501160426
43193CB00014B/2558